The Art Of Creative Drawing

Contents

Introduction

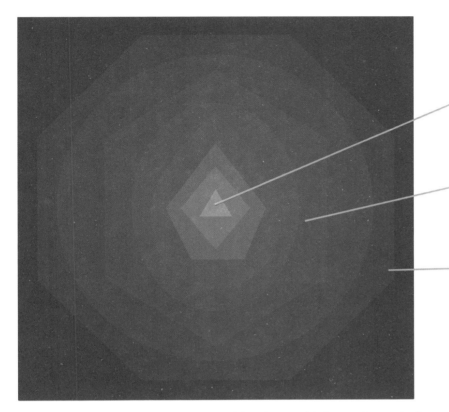

This image shows the three principle cycles revealed within the relationship between static and dynamic shapes.

- Dynamic triangular shapes in the centre, when coloured red or magenta represent creative activity.

- Static shapes such as hexagons coloured blue signifies structure and purpose.

- Balance is achieved by using both static and dynamic shapes and the colour violet.

The series has several primary objectives which are intended to assist the practitioner in developing more creative thought and application. These unique elements and combinations, whilst unusual, have been developed from early cultures such as Tibetan, American Indian, Arabic, Mayan and Indian.

Working with animals and plant symbols, geometric shapes and structure, together with the nature of colour, these art works are refreshingly inspirational. The majority of these pieces are produced within mandalas. The mandala dates back centuries and is known to cover all continents.

The purpose of the mandala is to explain mythological stories and culturally distinctive artwork. Unlike western art, as we understand it, these pieces derive from the natural world and spiritual understanding.

Each element of a mandala has meaning and represents some guiding aspects or principle. Geometry and placement of animal symbols play a significant part in explaining quite intricate elements and colour is used to structurally enhance, not simply embellish.

This series will inevitably educate and enthrall all age groups ranging from early teenage through to advancing years.

Things You Will Need

To complete the exercises in this book you will need some simple drawing tools. Most of these are inexpensive, easy to obtain and include basic equipment such as pencils, eraser, transparent ruler, compass and paper. As you become confident with your drawing skills there is no end to the creative ways you can colour your designs and your local art supplier will be able to advise you on the available range of quality paper and colouring pencils, markers and paints.

Compass: for drawing circles and aligning curved shapes. Look for one which allows you to change the pencil and thereby incorporate coloured pencils and markers.

Eraser: a good quality soft white eraser is preferable as it will help keep clean paper .

Ruler: for drawing straight lines and making accurate measurements. A transparent plastic ruler is most effective as it allows you to align your measurements with other shapes.

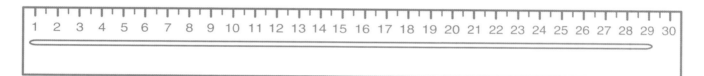

Paper: for practise and drawing your finished designs clean white A4 size sheets of bond paper are ideal; however for a better finish you may wish to use a quality art paper.

Pencils: for drawing your designs, including guidelines and outlines. Graphite pencils are preferred, particularly the HB grade as this is neither too dark nor light and can easily be erased. Coloured pencils are ideal for defining and colouring your finished designs. Harder art quality pencils are better for defining lines and edges while soft pencils are preferable for a smooth finish.

How to Use This Book

The Art of Creative Drawing series has been designed using both traditional freehand and geometric drawing methods. Innovative exercises are aimed at awakening your artistic potential through the creative use of lines, shapes, symbols and geometry. Although this is fundamentally a drawing book, colour has been added to highlight the symbolic qualities of different shapes and images.

General Drawing Tips

- For each exercise A4 size paper is recommended, though once feeling confident mandalas can be created to any size. Drawing at a larger scale simply requires extensions of established proportions.

- For each exercise we recommend drawing a square 180mm x180mm to act as an outer border. Exact measurements for creating each design are given. Where visual examples are enlarged (to highlight a step) or reduced (to see the bigger picture) simply follow the written instructions. Examples on page 14 show how shapes and sizes can be increased.

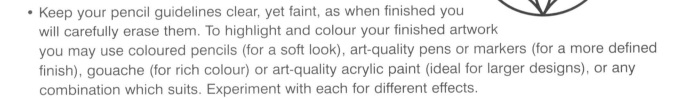

- When drawing new shapes and symbols you might like to practise on a separate sheet of paper until pleased with the result (this can save unnecessary pencil lines and erasing). Using a separate sheet also allows to trace your image a number of times until you are confident when drawing more spontaneously. This is particularly important where repetition and symmetry is needed.

- If you have trouble seeing through the paper when tracing images hold it up to the light, against a window or active computer screen.

- Keep your pencil guidelines clear, yet faint, as when finished you will carefully erase them. To highlight and colour your finished artwork you may use coloured pencils (for a soft look), art-quality pens or markers (for a more defined finish), gouache (for rich colour) or art-quality acrylic paint (ideal for larger designs), or any combination which suits. Experiment with each for different effects.

Drawing Circles and Squares

- Drawing circles and squares with a ruler or compass is the most accurate and precise method. However, most of the colouring designs were composed freehand.

Using What You Learn

- The information and exercises in this book lay the foundation for learning to draw mandalas. While there are guidelines to help you create symbolically rich designs there are no firm rules. There is no end to the wide range of designs you can create. Part of learning to draw is using your imagination and trusting yourself. More than anything the drawing experience should be enjoyable. Allow yourself to be open and experiment.

Exercise 1: The Form of Creation

Within this exercise we explore a Yantra (explained page 9) encapsulating inspirational energies. The intention being to activate and awaken creativity with the realisation that more is to be gained than viewing a piece of artwork.

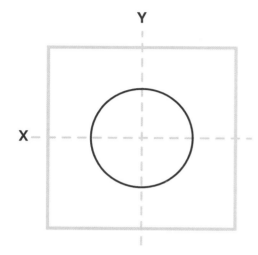

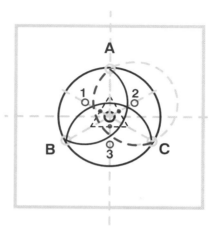

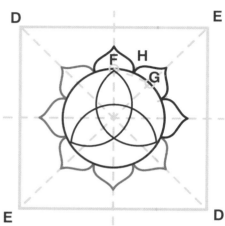

Illustrations not to scale

Step 1: Draw a square 180mm x 180mm, faintly add in the midlines for the vertical (Y) and horizontal (X) axis to obtain the centre point. Placing a compass in the centre draw a circle approximately 100mm in diameter. The square referring to the earth and the circle being creative potential.

Hints

Draw all lines and images faintly in pencil until satisfied with the final design.

Erase all guidelines before adding colour with pencils, inks or paints. It is important to keep the drawing faint by using a sharp pencil.

Step 2: Now place a small triangle in the centre by lightly tracing its outline from the archetypal shapes on page 14. (represented by the smaller dotted triangle). Draw a faint line from each corner of the triangle through the middle of the opposite side, extending each line to the perimeter of the circle. This will create points A, B and C. Connect points A to B, B to C, and C to A with the semi-circular lines. To do this find the resting point of the compass (points 1, 2 & 3) by measuring 28mm from the centre along the A, B, and C lines. Carefully erase the smaller triangle and guidelines.

Step 3: Draw two faint diagonal lines, to join opposite corners of the square through the centre (lines D and E). These form the remaining midlines for adding the outer petals. Rule a line from the top of the circle (F) to where the diagonal line on the right meets the circle (G). Measure halfway along the line and mark the petal on the circle (H). Measure 25mm from the circle along all midlines to mark the tips of the petals. Starting at the tip of the upper petal (above point F) draw a curved line to point H, then symmetrically draw the next line to the next tip (above point G). Aim to make the lines as even as possible either side of the midlines. Repeat this process to complete the remaining petals.

Step 4: The final image can be coloured in subtle variations of light blue and violet tones. Generally the main triangular shape referring to life force and creativity in action should be a magenta or bright violet. The other colours can alternate between light blue and violet tones giving an expansive effect.

To the left is the creation pattern known as the Tara Yantra. Traditional colours for the yantra can be seen on the inside front cover. Violet is sometimes used for its expansive effect. These colour combinations can apply to both images. The image in exercise one is a similar version of a contemporary Tara Yantra.

Symbolism

The Yantra is a symbolic form which explores various archetypal influences in nature. For example, the nine major planets each have Yantras associated with their specific forces while concurrently being part of the collective group or solar system. Deities are also ascribed certain yantras which, through form and colour, represent the expression of each deity's influence in life.

The TARA YANTRA is the form associated with the personified deity–Goddess Tara–which means shining or guiding light. It depicts the inspirational and activating energies of nature.

Fundamental Shapes

The three main modes of nature are active (dynamic), neutral (balancing) and passive (static). These principles can be applied in artwork. Often revealed with the colours red, white and blue. Red is associated with our desire to create. White is balancing and associated with equilibrium. This can also be represented by a gentle violet achieved when red and blue are combined. Deep blue and black symbolise the opposite polarity of pacifying and stable energies (dark blue) and inertia and stillness (black).

Active Dynamic Shapes

These shapes have active qualities relating to red and magenta. The first ellipse shape can be found in the forms of leaves and flowers for growth, fertility and inspiration. The second petal shape represents the unfolding and awakening of life energy. The triangle, the most dynamic is for creative desire and aspiration. The diamonds form a bridge between the triangle and pentagon signifying beginnings and expansion. The pentagon represents material creation and the principle of intercommunion.

Neutral Balancing Shapes

These shapes are for equalising, or neutral effect and for this reason are shown in white and violet. Together with light blue and soft pink these shapes range from being gently passive to gently active in nature, with the central soft violet, a neutral balance. Each refers to neutrality, fullness and harmony, preservation and refined thought.

Passive Static Shapes

These shapes have pacifying qualities and work closely with the colour blue. This passive mode of nature becomes represented when it deepens beyond the electric mid-blue tones to become a deeper and much darker shade. Dark indigo and purple are both associated with this cycle of nature. The mid-blue to the left symbolise general calmness and consolidation. The mid-deep blue tones, structure and universality (octagon) while the deep blue tones, destruction and dissolution (inverted triangle) and inertia and stillness (square).

Here we have many of the shapes from the previous page associated with three principle cycles reflecting an evolving relationship between static and dynamic shapes. Active dynamic triangular shapes are used in the centre with red and magenta for creative activity. Passive static shapes are used towards outer fringes with blues representing, structure and purpose. The point of balance is within the hexagonal and oval shapes and the colour violet. Including particular shapes into artwork adds further emphasis, particularly when related colours are used.

The Process of Creation

This image refers to creation entirely within a geometric form. It endeavours to show physical emergence from the centre as it encompasses shapes reflecting natural principles of expansion, restricted expression and structure. The colours, similar to the Tara Yantra in the first exercise, promotes gentle expansion and harmony for refined expression. The design includes some archetypal shapes associated with the process of creation, each represented on the opposite page.

Shapes and Their Processes — The Act of Creating from Nothing

Here are a range of shapes, each of which has a special significance in relation to the emergence of life force energies.

 The small circle or bindu shape (associated with Hindu culture) is the origin or source and therefore represents harnessed potential. It is often coloured black or deep blue to depict the embryo, unmanifested states and infinity. When symbolising a state of manifestation it is coloured white.

 The crescent or nada shape represents the act of creation and its emergence in the cycle of growth. This part circle shape is evident in the phases of the moon on its twenty eight day cycle.

 The oval, or cosmic egg (lingam shape) is found within many mythological images and tells of the formless assuming form. A primary shape in the process of creation (together with the circle) represents both the embryo and womb. When positioned vertically it also represents the generating principle of life.

 The teardrop or mitre shape represents the emerging form from the womb. In this regard it relates to deep blue and purple, signifying a life force emerging from the depths of darkness or undefined space. Often used to represent the ether element which can be white, to suggest expansion.

 The characteristics of the triangle are activity, initiation and creative desire, relating to bright red tones and the fire element. Although in pink and magenta it suggests more refined or gentler attributes. It represents a generating action and is appropriate for fostering inspiration in artwork.

 The hexagram (star-shaped hexagon) represents the balance between ascending (creative) and descending (destructive) forces associated with, and symbolises, preservation. Principles of balance, harmony and beauty are coloured aqua, violet, green and soft grey. It can also represent sustenance and the life-giving nature of the air element.

 The downward pointing triangle, when coloured black usually means descension or destruction. Depending on the colour, and as an example, red increase the ability for change in a destructive manner. Violet tones indicate gentler and more positive energies in this process while deep purple and blue represent regression.

 The square shape is of the earth element and appropriately adds fixed structure and foundation to artwork which is commonly created within a square or rectangle. The square refers to solidness and practicality, particularly with deep-blue and black colours. Using yellow it supports an expansive approach.

Archetypal Shapes

When the geometric shapes (triangle, square, pentagon etc.) are placed within a circle they provide an ideal foundation from which to design a mandala. Use any one of these shapes when wishing to construct balanced and symmetrical designs.

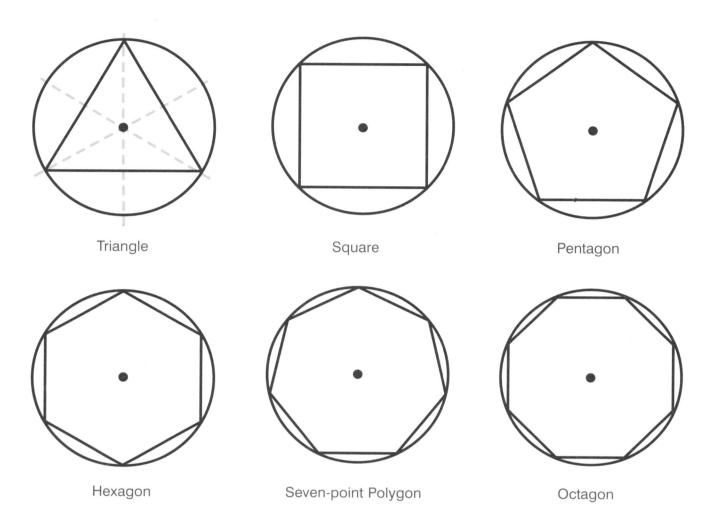

| Triangle | Square | Pentagon |

| Hexagon | Seven-point Polygon | Octagon |

For smaller-sized mandalas simply trace any of the above templates (as in the exercise on the next page.) Enlarging these templates will allow any required format.

Enlarging base archetypal shapes

Rule lines from the centre point to each outer point of your shape extending each line as far as you wish (in this example we are enlarging our base shape by 20mm). Measure 20mm from each outer point along each line creating your extended size. Join these points to create new shape. To complete a base, use your compass to contain the original shape with a circle. This method can be used to expand any original artwork.

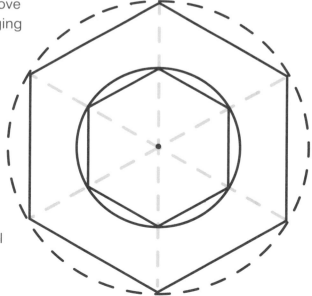

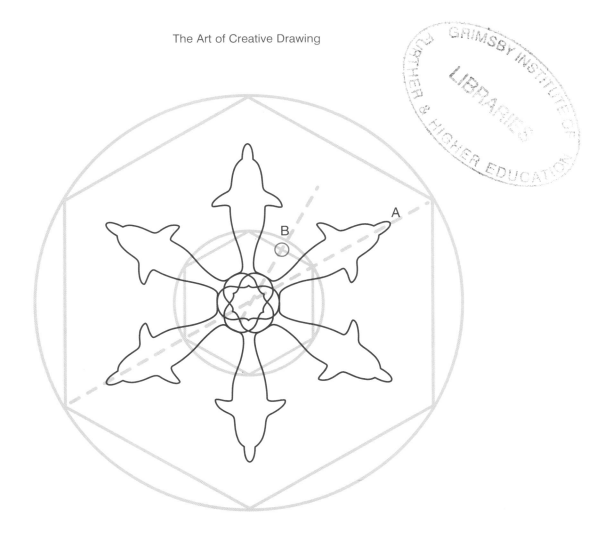

The following few pages illustrate and explain how an archetypal shape can be used as a base template for a mandala. By measuring equal distances from the centre, the smaller base shape can be easily enlarged. Central guidelines can either run through the main corner points (A) or be drawn halfway between the main lines (B).

Below are two further examples how shapes from the previous page extended can act as base structures for mandalas.

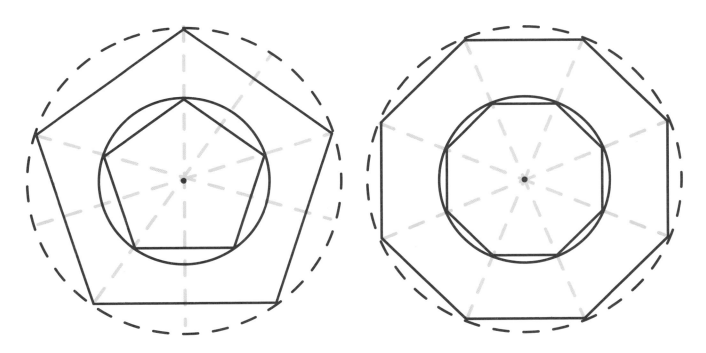

Exercise 2: The Birth of Form

This exercise explains when joining colours, shapes, symbols and totems they can reveal the birth of form. Composed entirely of curved lines reflecting the principle of balance it will help develop freehand drawing skills.

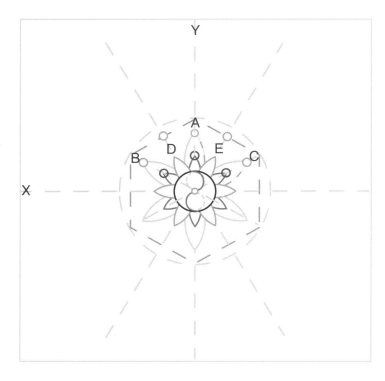

Step 1: Draw a square 180mm x 180mm and faintly add the midlines for the vertical (Y) and horizontal (X) axis to obtain the centre point. Draw a small circle 12mm in diameter in the centre. Then two smaller circles inside. Darken the right side of the top circle and the left side of the bottom circle to create a symmetrical figure-eight style curved line.

Step 2: Lightly trace the hexagon template from page 14. Mark the main guides from the centre through each corner point (A, B and C) and the mid-line guides halfway along (D, E and X) as shown on the left. Then draw the three six-pointed star shapes in the centre using the following measurements:

Star 1
(smallest star on main A-C lines):
11mm long, 3mm wide.
Star 2
(middle star on D, E, X lines):
12mm long, 4mm wide
Star 3
(largest star on main A-C lines):
18mm long, 5mm wide.

Step 3: The surrounding oval shape features the F, G, H and I points as guides.
The oval is 40mm wide and 50mm high in proportion with other shapes. Measure half this width on either side of the centre line and draw the joining curves freehand one quarter at a time. Using a compass to draw the outer circle 154 mm in diameter.

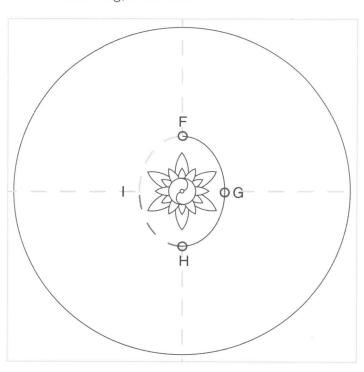

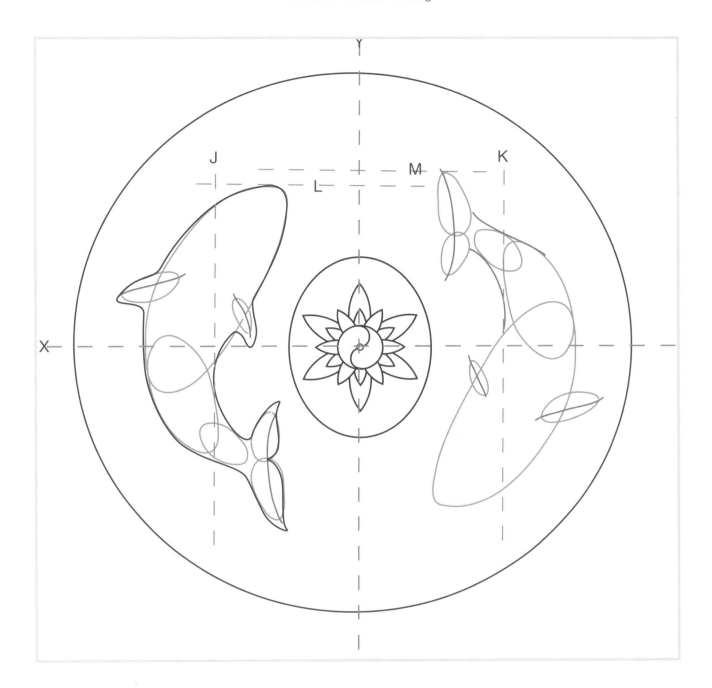

Step 4: Faintly draw the rough overlapping oval shapes for the whales in approximately the same positions as shown (light violet shapes). To align the shapes and obtain a better design it is useful to add guidelines on the X and Y axis. Measure 40mm along the X axis either side of the centre and draw two vertical lines for the approximate centre of each whale's body (J and K). Then measure along the Y axis 48mm (where the nose starts) and 56mm (where the tail ends) with two horizontal lines either side of the centre (L and M). These measurements are intended as guides only. The image illustrates approximate size and portion.

Step 5: Draw the final stylised whales as shown by the darker outline. Starting with the left place the inside fin on the X axis. Then draw down towards the inside tail by following the contours of the ovals. Finish the shape by copying the general curves. To duplicate, rotate the paper 180 degrees and repeat the same process using rough anchor points and curves for a freehand image. Erase the underlying shapes when this stage is finished.

Step 6: Draw the wavy ocean line across the horizontal axis. Then the two smaller circles representing the sun and moon each 20mm in diameter. To do this measure 46mm from the centre along the vertical Y axis to mark the centre point for each smaller circle (N and O). Finally, draw the outer circle 162mm wide.

Finishing Tips

Erase lines no longer needed. When satisfied with the image use ink pens or felt pens to make lines more permanent for colouring. If colouring the image with paints is preferred then pencil outline only. Be careful to erase all unwanted lines as these may show through.

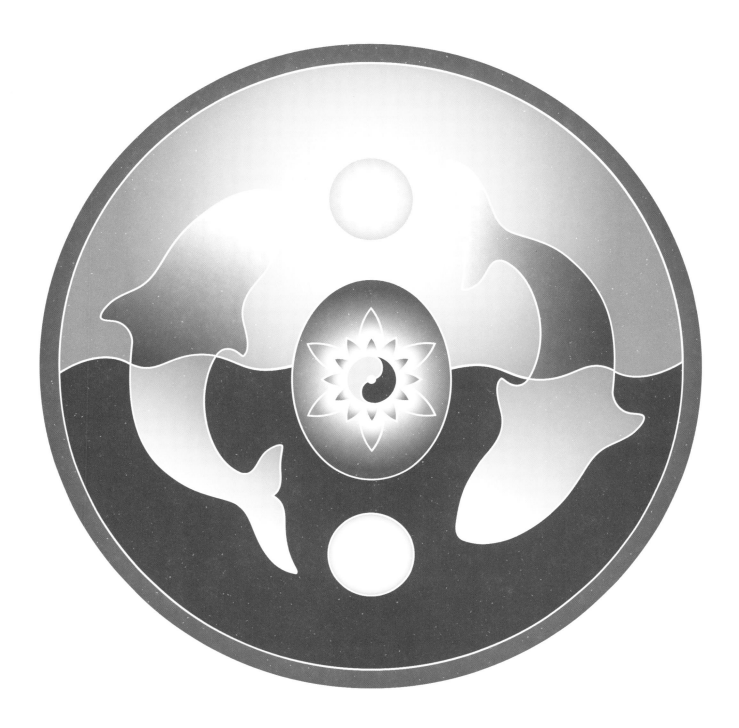

Colour plays a most important role in the final version of this mandala featuring the whale as its central totem. Representing the birth of form, these dedicated colours symbolise the womb of creation, peace and gestation (darker blue), openness and expansiveness (lighter blue), refined sensitivity and water (aqua), purity and birth (white), transformation and harmony (violet). The image also reflects polarity and balance represented by the sun and moon and the emerging and submerging motions of the whales. The overall effect is one of gentle movement depicted by the cyclic action of the whales and colouring being both passive and neutral.

Colour in Creation

Colour plays a vital role in art, drawing on emotions and feelings. Most cultures appreciate the role colour plays, using it symbolically in both artwork and traditional stories. For example yellow and red often represent qualities of expansion and vitality associated with the sun, while deep blue and black symbolise qualities of passivity and dissolution referring to the ocean and deep space. These pages offer a guide to colour usage, closely associated with animals, directions and elements which in themselves reveal unique characteristics.

White

White is associated with unity and purity as it reflects all other colours equally. It relates to the mutable and receptive qualities of nature therefore being associated with water, the Moon and Venus. White can be used to lighten images and relates well to all geographic directions, especially the north-west and the east in association with principles of birth, nurturance, abundance, peace and purity. Shapes suiting white are spherical and semi-circular. Animals reflecting white qualities are the deer (purity), swan (grace), cow (nurturance) and dove (peace).

Violet

Violet is considered the highest frequency of light in the colour spectrum and often used to depict qualities such as harmony, grace, refinement and transcendence. In its brighter tones violet can represent fiery energy and in its middle or lighter tones is warm or neutral, more refined and gentler. Shapes appropriate for violet are conical, fan, oval and the hexagon through the principle of harmony. Animals and birds suited to violet are the hummingbird (joy), dove (refinement), swan (grace), phoenix (transformation) and other birds, such as the parrot (freedom).

Magenta

Magenta is similar to the warmer violet colours and when brighter is often referred to as hot pink. This intensity can be found in many flowers as with the rising and setting sun. Magenta is appropriate for the transformation of life energies, such as the sun emerging into the light of a new day. In this regard it refers to vitality and inspiration. Preferred shapes for magenta are elliptical and fan, flame and triangular, and nine-sided stars and polygons. Animals reflecting magenta qualities are the butterfly (new life and aspiration), phoenix (transformation), horse (power and vitality) and bat (renewal).

Red

Red represents activating energies of nature such as desire, motivation, generation and manifestation. Red tends to have a warming effect and forms the basis for acceleration. Is often associated with fertility and initiating energies and reflecting the principles of motivation and desire promotes creativity. Shapes best expressed by red are triangular and fiery designs. Animals reflecting qualities associated with red are the horse (power and vitality), ram (assertiveness) and rooster (pride).

Orange

Orange is the bridge between red and yellow; a warm colour conveying gentle or refined activity. In bright shades, ideally suiting to the sun (such as at sunrise or sunset) depicting inspiration. In pastel tones it has nurturing and sustaining qualities of the moon, the light of the sun in a cooler subdued state. Gold-orange tones are expansive and aligned with the earth element. Whereas red-orange tones the fire element representing the generating principle. The best shapes are the diamond and square. Animals reflecting orange qualities are tiger (devotion) and ram (assertiveness).

Yellow

Yellow suits expansion and growth and gives a warm, enlivening effect. Used to create stimulation it works with images depicting the awakening of life energy, such as the dawn and early morning. In this regard yellow maintains a strong connection with the east, ranging from the north through the east to the south. Shapes appropriately coloured yellow are ellipses, diamonds and the square conveying fertility and expansion into manifestation. Animals and birds associated with yellow are the hummingbird (joy), the coyote (play), parrot (freedom) and bee (fertility).

Green

Green quite naturally is for preservation, growth and renewal and effectively used with both symbols and images depicting growth and fertility. As it is the middle colour in the spectrum, green defines communication and balance and combines well with most other colours. In its lime shades it adds warmth to an image while in aqua shades, coolness. It relates to the air element through the principle of sustenance and to the earth with growth and fertility. Appropriate shapes are the pentagon and hexagon, showing aspects of communication and represent growth and balance. The turtle (fertile aspect of earth/communion), parrot (growth and expression), peacock (preservation) and dragon (fertility) are each suited to the colour green.

Blue

Blue conveys calmness, peace and stillness. Darker blues represent inertia and have the most passive and supportive effect on their environment. The lighter blues are also gently passive and imply expansiveness, as seen in the light and pastel blue tones of the morning sky. Therefore darker blue tones relate to the west; lighter to the north for expansiveness. The octagon (deep blue) and passive circles and semi-circles (mid and lighter blues) are ideal shapes. Deep blue relates to the water element and gestation creating new life. Light blue relates to the air element symbolising the open sky, while very light blue is associated with the subtlest element, ether. Animals and birds seen in deep and mid blue qualities are whales (birth of form), the dolphin (communication) and for pastel blue qualities, the otter (expansion and play) and doves (peace).

The Symbolism of Creation Emerging

The below symbols or stylised pieces of art are both useful and harmonious within mandalas. The traditional approach logically suggest starting the design at the centre and expanding outwards, mirroring the gradual emergence of growth. Rich symbolism is contained in these shapes and designs can be simple or elaborate depending on skills and inspiration.

A significant central symbol the bindu represents the void and the source from which all creation emerges. It represents origin—the centre—and the essence of animated form. Deep blue and black are its suited colours.

The diamond eye reveals a window into the unknown. Also symbolises the opening to the dream state of consciousness known as the astral plane.

The lingam or cosmic egg symbol represents the formless assuming form, the unknown becoming known. The infinite, the creative principle, the beginning and the end. Symbolic of totality and completeness it represents the generating force within creation. Suited to gold and purple tones.

The snake is a symbol of cosmic feminine energy and raw potential. Together with fertility, it represents hidden and unseen energies in nature rising to the light of day. Relating to the colour black it associates with unknown or latent energy aspects, with red and magenta both will and transformation.

Inherent powers of the trinity are reflected in the trident. Three worldly planes (earth, astral and causal) and three modes of nature (activity, tranquillity and inertia). Timelessness and nonattachment to the past, present and future. Characteristically triumphant it relates well to gold or violet colourings.

Representing the awakening, unfolding energies in creation the lotus largely depicts the heart centre. Other aspects are purity, and reaching into higher knowing. Mostly pastel tonings for colouring, magenta for inspiration, white for purity, and blue for newly formed potential.

The water element is often seen as a half-full/half-empty shape symbolising balance. Sometimes depicted by rippling effects illustrated in some of the following mandalas. Nature's wonderful resource it is seen as continual movement of life in a peaceful and balanced way. Blue tones, particularly aqua blue are appropriate colours.

Creative Colouring

The following pages give an opportunity for colouring various mandalas. These can be traced or enlarged. Refer to guides in previous pages or the back of the book when experimenting with different colours and shadings.

This image is symbolic of creation emerging from original or cosmic waters, a concept represented in many ancient, as well as modern, cultural traditions. This particular image is a contemporary version incorporating a range of symbols and principles. the overall effect is in harmony although incorporating both active, (seen as dynamic generating shapes) and the more passive (curved and softer lines)

Here is a simple depiction of the emergence of the life force and conception of form. Created from the centre point this image is in a state of flux/movement until it reaches the lotus petals around the edge where it shows a more solid structure. Harmonious balance between the inner fluid energies and the outer octagonal shape forming its boundaries.

The winged scarab, a traditional totem from Egypt symbolising the awakening of creation and the dawn of a new day. An empowering image depicting balance between the solar/lunar, masculine/feminine or light/dark polarities in life.

The peacock represents the glory of material creation and is traditionally associated with the principle of preservation. The overall energies of this mandala are balancing yet it shows as a dynamic effect with flowing water and the vitality of the sun.

Creation Symbols from Various Cultures

In cultures throughout the world symbols play an important role in art and creation stories, representing qualities such as growth, and expansion. Throughout the centuries symbols have formed a common language communicating the very essence of creative processes. Below are a few symbols used around the world, representing fundamental aspects, such as creative and destructive forces, duality, balance and life everlasting.

Symbols for the four directions are commonly found in Native American traditions with each culture having slight variations. The symbol on the left is the Hopi symbol for connecting the Earth to the Spirit realm. The second is the Wakan Tanka (or Great Mystery), which represents creation spiralling into manifestation.

The above two variations of cosmic energy found originally amongst Indian and Tibetan traditions, symbolise anti-clockwise and clockwise movement representing the constructive and destructive forces of creation. They also represent cosmic male and female energies of creation.

In Egyptian tradition the ank is a symbol for the continuation of time, everlasting life and immortality. In the language of shapes it is a combination of the cross and a figure eight, an ongoing cycle or eternity. These are both powerful references to life and truth.

In the Celtic, Druid and Christian traditions the cross is depicted in a variety of ways, such as the two shown above. They represent the merging of opposite polarities, such as life and death or the material and the spiritual, represented by the horizontal and vertical axis. It is also associated with the principles of sacrifice, surrender and truth.

The Yin Yang symbol is associated with Asian traditions such as Taoism, Feng Shui and other aspects of contemporary Chinese and Japanese culture. Here the duality principle represents harmony and balance between opposites, such as male and female, day and night, and the sun and moon. The two dots also form a cross when joined.

A variety of cross symbols are found in the Meso-American traditions of the Mayan and Aztec people. Basic crosses depicting the four directions are common, as are designs incorporating spirals and crosses. These are drawn on ceremonial shields and found throughout their artwork.

Exercise 3: Myths, Legends and Creative Stories

This exercise once again represents the emerging energies of nature in the style of the Native American Indian tradition. Although chosen symbols and animal totems compliment this theme you may experiment further with variations using this basic structure as a central foundation.

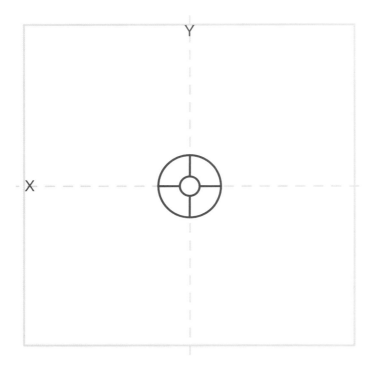

Step 1: Draw a square 180mm x 180mm and faintly add the midlines for the vertical (Y) and horizontal (X) axis to obtain the centre point. Placing a compass in the centre draw two small circles approximately 8mm and 22mm wide. Connect these two circles along the X and Y axis lines. This central shape is the Native American Indian symbol for Mother Earth representing the four sacred directions and seasons.

Step 2: Draw the four pedestal shapes. Start three faintly horizontal lines across the Y axis line 22mm wide (11mm either side of the line), 18mm (A), 26mm (B) and 30mm (C) from the centre. Next, two vertical lines 6mm either side of the Y axis (D and E) for the inner edge of the pedestal. Draw the pedestal outline as highlighted. Repeat this process for the other three shapes. The pedestals reveal the sacred seat for the animal totems and four directions which representing diversity.

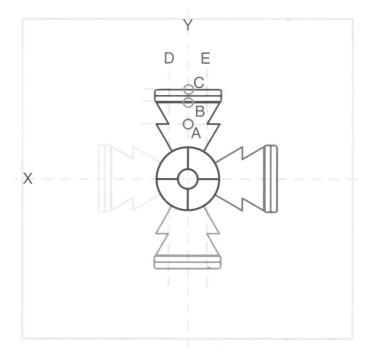

Remember
East in traditional mandalas is often located at the top.

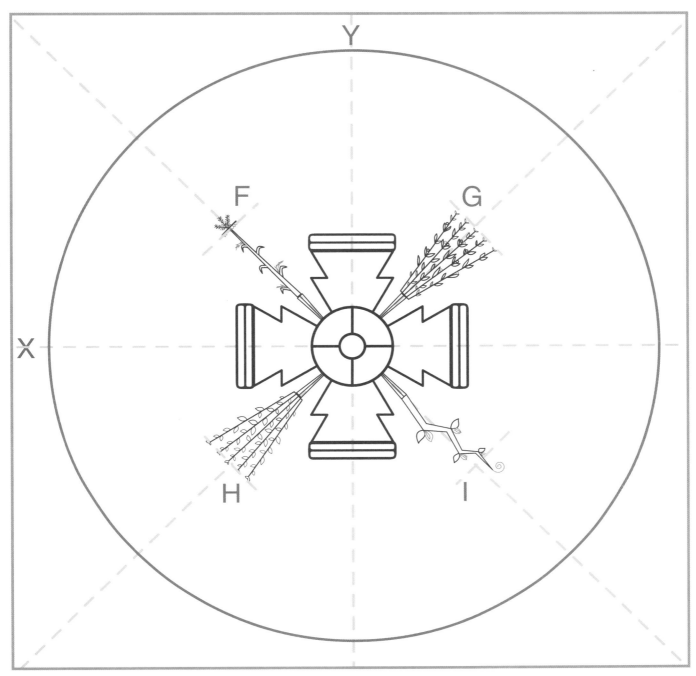

Step 3: Anchoring a compass in the centre draw an outer circle approximately 152mm wide. Next the plants related to the four directions, sacred plants associated with the Navaho tradition: corn, tobacco, squash and bean plants—refer to box for symbolism. Start by drawing faintly the two diagonal lines joining opposite corners of the square. Measure approximately 60mm from the centre along each line, making small guidelines for the tip of each plant (F, G, H, I). Then add the plants as shown starting with corn in the top left corner. As these are only interpretations, simple outlines are adequate.

In Native American Indian tradition corn represents fertility and is a primary source of food. Associated with ceremony and prayer, tobacco is another sacred plant, believed to connect the physical and celestial realms. Storing water in the hot summer months the squash plant is symbolic of sustenance, and the bean plant, a primary source of protein, sacred to survival.

Step 4: Finally, draw the animal totems in simple outline. Practise using the animals from the previous exercise, or experiment with other animals of choice or those on the following page. Choosing animals which compliment the intended cultural theme, seasons, environment and directions as it is important they align their attributes and energy with the symbolic nature within the mandala. As animal totems represent characteristics of the group psyche on a celestial level this will positively reflect in your abilities to feel for the subject. Placing animals at random or perhaps even in conflict positions will disrupt the visual effect. The above animals have been chosen for the southern hemisphere where the sun travels across the north—refer to box for symbolism.

The eagle represents illumination and the awakening of a new day. The owl, power to see beyond the darkness, associated with night in the southern hemisphere. The turtle, earth energies for consolidation and integration of the day passing into dusk. The dolphin, peaceful and playful energies, an ideal totem for the northern direction in the southern hemisphere. Other animal totems can be added to outside borders, complementing the design.

This image represents a creation story from the Navaho Indians of the Central Plains. Colours strongly associated with many Native American tribes are red, white, blue, black and yellow, though they vary from tribe to tribe relative to the vision or story being depicted. For the Navaho the four sacred colours relating to the four directions are white for east (dawn), blue for south (day in the northern hemisphere), yellow for west (dusk), and black for north (night). The mythical stylised figure around the outer circle represents the rainbow goddess central to their culture. The coyote, a common totem associated with the emergence of time and new beginnings representing dawn. The swallow represents the day energies of creation, playfulness and joy. The frog is the transformation of the day's experiences; the joining of day and night (dusk). The snake, hidden unknown energies of creation associated with the night.

Colours and Animal Totems

Here are examples of colour relating to specific animals whilst reflecting their intrinsic qualities. Using colour with animal totems is a powerful form of expressing qualities in art.

Eagle

The eagle, a symbol of freedom and realisation is often depicted. Representing an easterly direction, associated with the awakening of life energies. Colours strongly connected are violets and yellow suggesting expansion and illumination.

Turtle

The turtle is often associated with the earth element in Dreamtime and mythological stories is appropriately coloured green, brown and black. In light blue and aqua the turtle affirms self-communion and self-expression, qualities naturally emanating from the water element. Strongly associated with the direction north.

Owl

The owls characteristics are mystery and magic with both feminine and lunar energies. Vision, insightful and intuitive, it is used as a totem to depict the unknown. The owl, sometimes linked with the east often represents the reflection of the sun's light by the moon. Together with to darker lunar qualities of the west and north-west.

Dolphin

The dolphin has a playful and communicative energy suggesting childlike and innocent qualities. It's blue tones endorse peace and aqua, freedom of expression and self-communion. As a totem it relates well to the north.

Bear

The bear symbolises the unconscious and the unknown aspects of life becoming realised. Its images are usually documented in deep purple and black colour tones. A bear totem inspires inner knowledge arising from the gestation period of the winter months and in this regard relates to the west. In the northern hemisphere more closely related to the north.

Whale

The whale, representing gestation and the birthing of creative potential emerging from a dark unknown. As a totem it refers to inert energies arising from darkness into the light. The appropriate colour is deep blue.

Exercise 4: The Spiral of Creation

In many creation stories the spiral symbolises the process of ones journey, moving in a revolving manner. The universe constructed from a spiral path creates new planets and many minerals and flowers, similarly evolving and growing spiral patterns. In this exercise we recreate the animal totems from the previous page reflecting that same spiral and spiritual path.

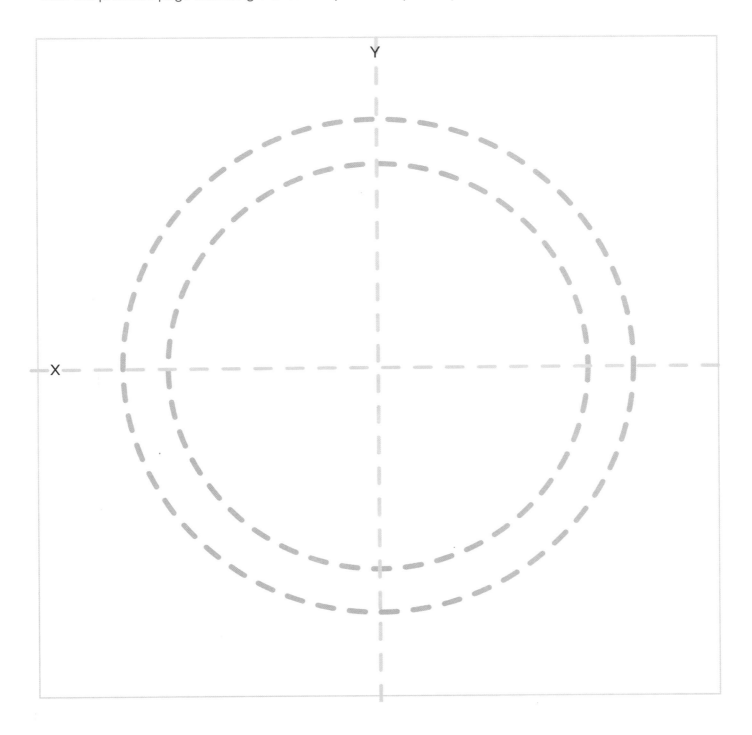

Step 1: Draw a square 180mm x 180mm faintly adding the midlines for the vertical (Y) and horizontal (X) axis to obtain the centre point. Place your compass in the centre and draw two faint circles 112mm and 136mm in diameter. Doing this, measure half these distances on the horizontal axis marking points at 56mm and 68mm either side of the centre. These two circles represent the womb of life forces.

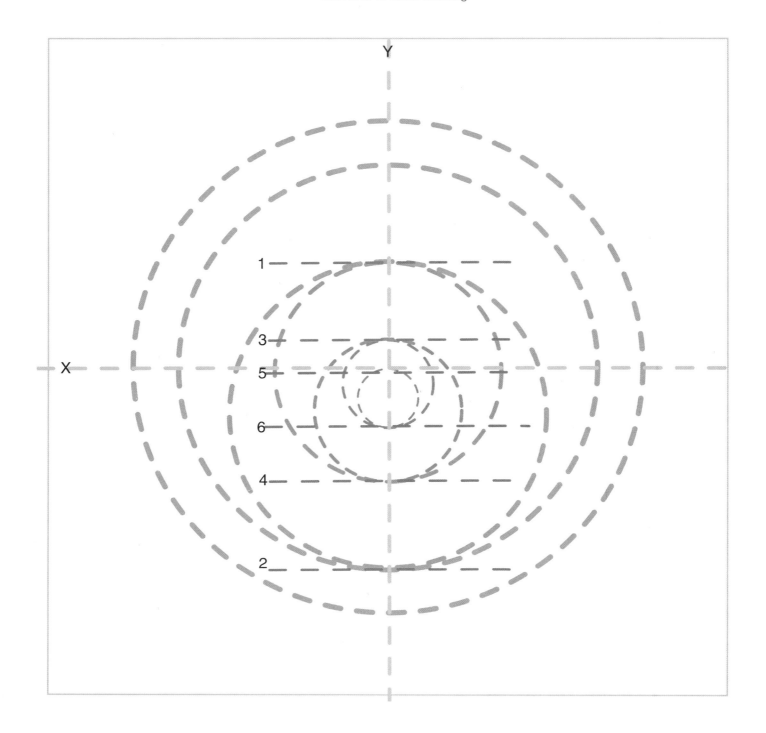

Step 2: Create faint guidelines for the upper and lower edges of the five inner circles as follows:

Line 1:   30mm up from the X axis (along the Y axis)
Line 2:   56mm down from the X axis (along the Y axis)
Line 3:   8mm up from the X axis (along the Y axis)
Line 4:   30mm down from the X axis (along the Y axis)
Line 5:   The X axis
Line 6:   16mm down from the X axis (along the Y axis line)

As these are only guidelines draw faintly. Drawing the circles in the next step after marking the centre point for each circle.

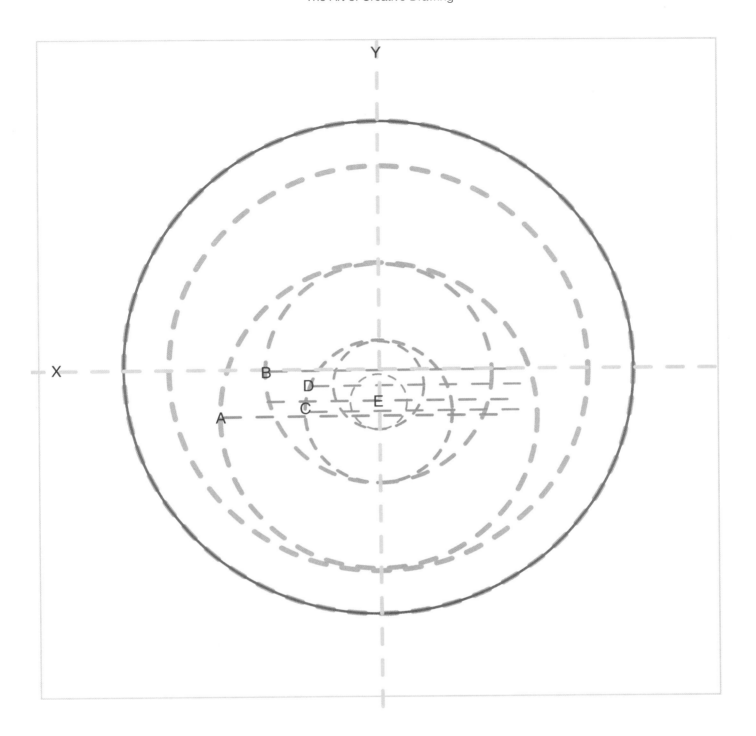

Step 3: Use the following measurements by marking the centre points A-E for the five inner circles:

Point A (centre of circle 1):   13mm down from the X axis along the Y axis (between lines 1 and 2)
Point B (centre of circle 2):   The X axis (between lines 1 and 4)
Point C (centre of circle 3):   12mm down from the X axis along the Y axis (between lines 3 and 4)
Point D (centre of circle 4):   4mm down from the X axis along the Y axis (between lines 3 and 5)
Point E (centre of circle 5):   8mm down from the X axis along the Y axis (between lines 5 and 6)

Place a compass on each of these points and join lines as indicated. Once again, keep the lines faint as these circles are purely guidelines for the final spiral pattern.

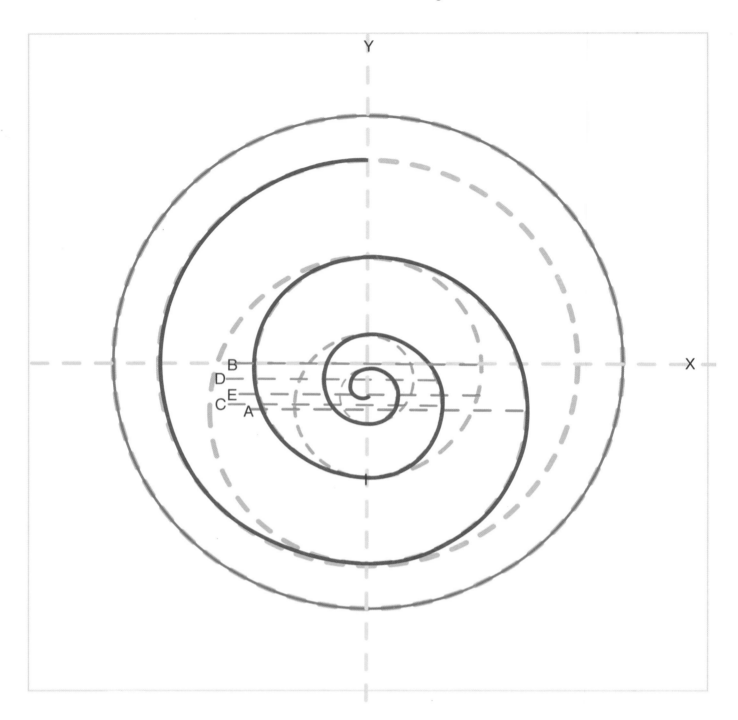

Step 4: Using the diagram as an indication draw the spiral shape over the six inner circles linking each in a clockwise direction. Starting at the centre of the smallest circle (E) draw a semi-circle curve clockwise to it's top, continue in this direction with the spiral effect following each circle and expanding to other lines. Then trace the opposite side of the next (larger) circle.

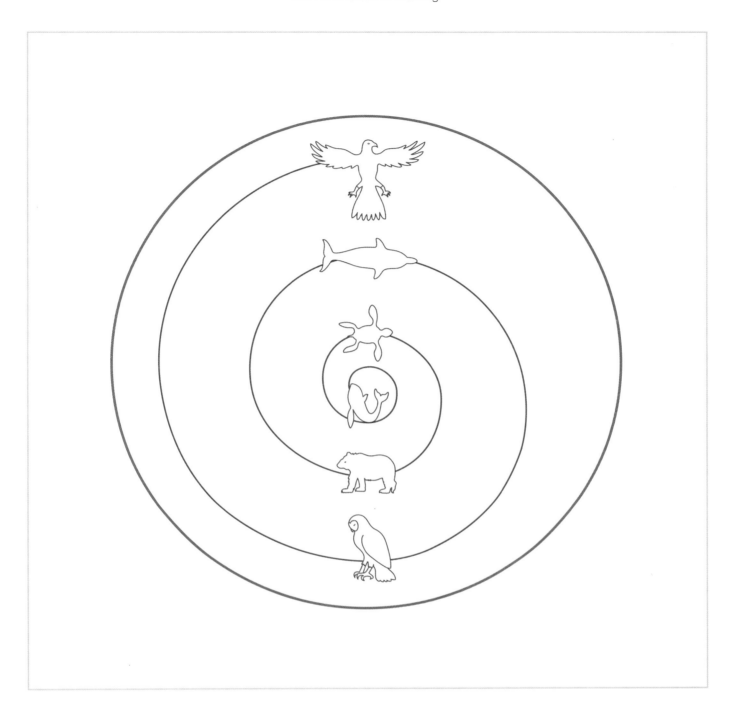

Step 5: Finally, draw the animal totem outlines featured on page 36, starting with the whale in the centre finishing with the eagle, again in a clockwise direction. As the totems are purely symbolic exact dimensions are not necessary. Practise by first copying or tracing on a separate sheet of paper, then add to the design. When finished carefully erase all guidelines and colour the image. The completed mandala is represented overleaf.

The previous steps are transformed into an art piece showing solid colour and a clever effect with dots. The deep blue tones indicate gestation and purpose while reflecting the emerging energies of the spiral. It also represents the whale, turtle and bear totems. As the colour expands to other fringes it supports all other elements. A further feature reveals the animals and birds at the lower section representing autumn and deep winter, whereas the animals at the top half, spring and summer, each reflecting a combination of colours and totem principles.

Exercise 5: Drawing Eagles

An ability to see animals in terms of their basic shapes assists the development of your drawing skills. In this exercise we feature four different birds, each distinct in outline and form.

Step 1: Firstly draw the faint outlines using oval shapes and curved lines. These provide a rough framework from which to continue.

Step 2: Next the basic outline of the eagle as depicted. The main intention, to emphasise where various shapes meet. Curves and points importantly giving the eagle its unique characteristics.

Step 3: The final stage to darken the more detailed lines, such as wings and tail. The shadow marks, as a rule appear on the underside with minimal shading on top creating a more realistic, three-dimensional effect.

Exercise 6: Drawing Doves

STEP 1: The faint outlines form the oval shapes and curved lines, providing a simple framework to develop further. As this is a symmetrical image, maintaining balanced guidelines on both sides is important.

Step 2: Create the basic outline of the dove. Again, paying attention to various shapes, curves and points giving the dove its unique characteristics.

Step 3: Finally, the more detailed stages for wings and tail. The shadow marks generally appear on the underside with minimal shading elsewhere.

Exercise 7: Drawing Owls

Step 1: Feature the faint outlines of the oval shapes and curved lines. The angle although similar to the earlier eagle is flying in the opposite direction. The owl being smoother and more feminine in its shape and general body lines.

Step 2: Next darken the basic outline. Curves and points importantly giving the owl its unique characteristics, represented here in a gentle gliding motion.

Step 3: Finally, the more detailed lines, such as wings and tail. Again, highlighting shadowed areas featured on the underside.

Exercise 8: Drawing Swans

Step 1: Starting with the faint outline of the oval shapes and curved lines, the swan has a graceful and pear-shaped body with predominantly feminine curved lines.

Step 2: Fill in the basic outline of the swan similar to the image shown. Where the neck meets the body it forms a figure eight shape helping align and balance the overall image.

Step 3: Finally, the more detailed lines, such as wings and underbelly, adding a more realistic three-dimensional effect.

Exercise 9: The Art of Peace

This exercise emphasises principles of peace and harmony shown by the dove and a seven-pointed star. Some interesting patterns and movements emerge between the inner and outer symbols.

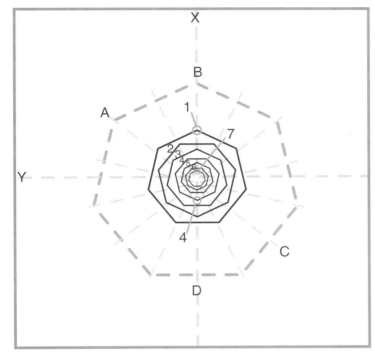

Step 1: Draw an outer square 180mm x 180mm adding faintly the midlines for the vertical (Y) and horizontal (X) axis to obtain the centre point. Then faintly trace the seven-sided polygon using the archetypal shapes on page 14 as a guide. Draw the main guidelines from corner points (such as A and B) through the centre to meet at the midpoint of the opposite side (as in points C and D).

Step 2: Using a sharp pencil draft the seven smaller polygons in the centre, rotating each one alternately, using the radius measurements from below (the distance from the centre to each corner point). It is not necessary to draw all seven (though these complement the mandala design). If seven is too difficult a lesser number is acceptable.

Polygon 1:   11 mm radius
Polygon 2:   9 mm radius
Polygon 3:   7 mm radius
Polygon 4:   5 mm radius
Polygon 5:   3.5 mm radius
Polygon 6:   3 mm radius
Polygon 7:   2 mm radius

Step 3: Draw two circles 96mm and 164mm wide. Extend the guidelines 25mm past the first circle to mark the tips and bases of the petals (E, F and G). Connect each consecutive tip and base point with curved lines as shown, while keeping them symmetrical (E to F, then F to G). Repeat this process for the remaining petals.

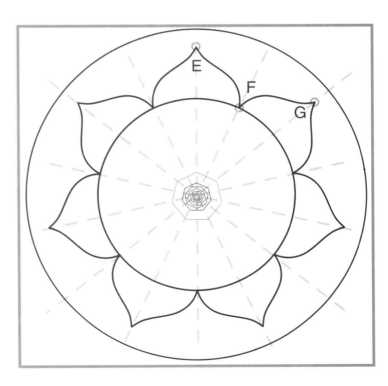

Step 4: Next include seven doves. Initially by drawing four faint horizontal lines across each main midline at 13mm (H), 25mm (I), 38mm (J) and 42mm (K) from the centre. These mark the tail line, mid point line, beak line and wing-tip line. If preferred, draw all guidelines before adding any of the doves. Now draw each bird's outline. Rotate the page making it easier to draw and maintain symmetry. You may prefer to simplify the tail and wings into one curved line. Once completed erase the faint horizontal guidelines except for the wing-tip line (K), which is used as a guideline for the next step, the heart shapes.

Step 5: Draw the seven inner heart shapes using the original guidelines (A and B) as centre lines. Firstly measuring 56mm along each line from the centre to mark the tip of the heart (L). Using the previous wing-tip line (K) as a baseline draw the heart shapes making them approximately 14mm wide. When drawing the seven outer heart shapes use the original midlines (M) as guides. Measure out 56mm along these lines to mark the tip point (N) and top line (O). Draw these approximately 14mm wide.

Step 6: After finishing the hearts in the larger circle draw the interwoven heart shapes in the four outer corners (P). Firstly extend a faint guideline from the centre to each corner. Measure out 92mm and 115mm to mark the top-line (Q) and tip point (R). Draw the outer heart shape 25mm wide. Using this as a guide draw a second smaller inverted one inside. Finally the third smaller heart shape, each connecting with the other in one continuous line. Repeat for each corner.

This final image reveals how effectively combined colour with geometric shapes, animal totems and symbols can create a gentle and softened effect. This mandala is alive yet peaceful as there is a balance of inward and outward pointing shapes within the display. Soft blue, light violet and white express particularly, qualities of freedom and unity. Shading from lighter to darker tones adds the illusion of gentle movement enhancing the overall symbolism, the emergence of peace and harmony.

Creative Colouring

The following pages allow an opportunity to colour various mandalas. These can be traced or enlarged. Refer to colour guides in previous pages or the back of the book and experiment with different colours and shadings.

Colouring Tips: The final image has been kept uncoloured allowing to use any one of a number of mediums and methods. Coloured pencils are suggested for creating a gentle shading effect (shown in the previous image). You may also darken the outlines of the design using ink, felt pens or coloured pen; either a standard ballpoint pen or fine marker is suitable. Alternatively, finish your design by applying solid colour with pencils, felt pen or paints. Decorating the design by drawing coloured dots along outlines as shown in Exercise 4, if the intention is to use paints use heavier paper.

This image depicts both duality and union. It has a clockwise flow and is symmetrically balanced from left to right and top to bottom. The whale figures represent birth—creation emerging and taking form with its qualities relating to deep blue. The conch shell represents unity and the call to remember the inter-connectedness of life. Soft pastel shades of blue and white are appropriate.

This feature shows lunar and feminine energies, moving and alive in its geometry and design. White for owls, represents luna energies with deep blues and purple tones for the night sky. The garland of jasmine flowers being white or pink, as are the roses contained within. The lingam, or cosmic egg shape, being garlanded is symbolic of feminine energies. Positioned vertically however, it suggests a masculine force and seed source.

This image represents four-fold principles of creation emphasising solidity, practicality and cohesion. The dragonfly symbolises change and dispelling of illusion, reflecting the transforming aspects of nature. The air and water elements relates well to soft pastel shades, specifically light blues and greens. The four conch shells represent purity and unity and signify the four directions of east, south, west, and north.

Ornamental Borders

Ornamental borders and patterns are a useful and recognisable way of depicting certain cultural and traditional art. From Celtic knotwork to Egyptian and Native Indian designs, there is a diverse range of border decorations and patterns which can be incorporated into artwork, many symbolising natural qualities.

A detailed border of classical Indian design.

Symbolising the planet Venus this border originates from Mayan culture.

A universal border design found throughout Egypt, India and Japan.

More universal border designs found throughout ancient Greece, Egypt and Tibet.

Exercise 10: Rectangular Border Design

Border designs, while appearing to be complex are often based on simple geometric guidelines. With a little patience and care, particularly when a border needs to flow evenly round corners and sides, impressive results can be achieved. This border exercise is based on straight lines and rectangular shapes.

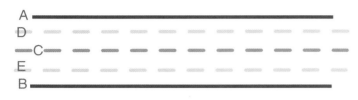

Step 1: Begin by faintly drawing a horizontal midline (C) 168mm wide across your page. Then two further horizontal lines 18mm either side (lines A and B) making them 36mm apart. Then add two more guidelines 10mm either side of the centre (D and E) 20mm apart.

Step 2: Draw the vertical lines between D and E with the main lines (F, G and H) 24mm apart. Start with the F line at 0mm (D to E), then draw the I line at 6mm across (E to C), the J line at 18mm (D to C) and then G at 24mm (D to E). Repeating this process for the entire border.

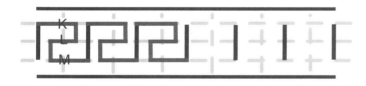

Step 3: Draw the horizontal lines K, L and M by connecting the missing space along the C, D and E lines, shown in magenta.

The finished version to the left is a border style used in ancient Greece. To achieve the slight variation in the last example follow the below instructions.

In this pattern simply omit and replace the centre line (C) with two new guidelines (N and O) 3mm above and below the centre. Extend the I line to the N, across 6mm, then down to the O line and across 6mm to the extended J line. Repeating for the rest of the border.

Egyptian artwork is well known for its ornate designs. These examples are variations of lotus borders symbolising interconnected life and growth. The last example is a simple border design used often for edging.

Border designs featured strongly in Celtic tradition are commonly based on the principle of knotwork, a simple overlapping and underlapping of lines (with no loose ends) allowing endless variations. Knotwork can be created from as little as two interweaving lines or with perhaps six or more lines as seen here.

Colour Qualities

This section explains the symbolic qualities associated with individual colours. Using and combining colours in thoughtful ways undoubtedly enhances the artwork.

White

White symbolises purity and liberation promoting energy and the highest potential. In Tantric art it represents the masculine aspect of a deity. It associates with water and often assigned to feminine planets such as the Moon and Venus, purifying and pacifying the emotions. White is often used to provide contrast and bridge other colours.

Violet

Violet is associated with harmony and when becoming more inert and as deep purple, in action it returns to its original source. In its mid tones it conveys neutrality and its brighter shades, higher transformation. In its light shades violet associates with tranquility and as darker purple, more deeply passive. This is a unique combination of the coming together of two opposite energies.

Magenta

In mandalas it is used to evoke the goddess. It is the passion and vitality of the creative force merged with the white and violet rays and signifies aspiration. Magenta is commonly used to colour triangles and the Sun.

Pink

Pink has a calming and harmonising effect of the emotions and promotes deeper creative urges. Pink can symbolise creativity manifesting and the potential for refined sensitivity. In mandalas pink is usually for gentle feminine energies and used for colouring auspicious goddesses, the Sun, the Moon, Mars and Venus merged in unison representing male and female balance.

Red

Red associates with desire, fertility and manifestation. In Tantric art it is used to represent the fire element and the feminine attributes of a deity. In association with astrological influences however, red relates to the masculine planets of Mars and the Sun (as fire red and magenta) are appropriate colour for triangles.

Orange

Orange is used to show the gentle masculine or feminine energies of the rising sun, the full moon (as pastel) and the energies of auspicious goddesses. Blended with golden yellows and pinks represents a gentle creative force. Pastel orange represents maternal and nurturing energies and is considered the more feminine or purer expression of the above.

Yellow

Yellow represents expansive qualities and is often used to colour the outer square or perimeter of a mandala. Also signifying the earth element. In its saffron tone it represents joy, abundance, general wealth and good fortune.

Gold

Golden tones in the tawny green-brown range are traditionally used to show negative and destructive energies of wrathful forces. Relating to murky colours, such as a swamp it promotes turbulent chaotic energies. Pure gold (metallic) in striking contrast depicts the highest of vibrations. Relating to perfection and transcendence it is used to emphasise shapes representing the highest virtues.

Lime

Lime is used for fertile and active life-giving energies, observing new growth and the vitality of spring. Lime can be used in the outer square for active and communicative life energies and has invigorating qualities. Lime has a vitalising and stimulating effect and generally only needs to be used in small amounts in artwork as it can be overpowering.

Green

Green, linked to lime, also fosters communication and exchange and reflects similar properties, such as growth and fertility. As mid-green it depicts interconnection and as a cooler emerald and blue-green shade implies calmness. Green is often used to signify the air element and the balancing aspect of nature as it can be either warm (active) or cool (passive).

Aqua

Although not traditionally used in the mandala this colour is effective when working with higher expression and harmony within the emotions. It fosters artistic freedom of expression and refined sensitivity. This colour suits the elements air and water.

Blue

Blue in its lighter tones is similar to aqua and can be found in some mandalas and yantras to represent gentle passive deities. It is symbolically used for the air element in light pastel blues promoting openness and expansiveness. Blue relates to gentle and refined expression and the energies coloured by the throat chakra.

Deep Blue

As the blue ray approaches its mid tones it starts relating to neutrality and passiveness. In traditional sacred art, blue is often used to reveal the qualities of structure and contraction (dark blue). Deep blue also relates to withdrawal, or receding and connecting with the life source vibration.

Indigo

Indigo represents integration, purposefulness and structural integrity and is utilised when defining boundaries. The most invigorating of the blue tones it promotes insight, relating to the light of life. In its deeper tones it encourages insight into more contemplative mysteries.

Black

Black defines the light and all other colours. It is used in mandalas for border designs and boundaries, representing structure. Through qualities of negativity and devolution it is also associated with the earth element. Black can be used to depict negative or wrathful energies, or inertia and darkness in general.

Grey

In its smoky colour grey is traditionally used in mandalas to depict the element ether. In its light smoky tones it is associated with air and to the unseen and invisible energies. Used in the mandala it emphasises both beauty and perfection.

Flower of Life Geometric Matrix

The creation mandala above is known as the 'Flower of Life' and is found throughout the world in a number of ancient temples. It shows flawless symmetry, geometric perfection and completeness, illustrating some of the base geometric patterns of nature. This image, together with its original seed form, the 'Seed of Life' (highlighted in the centre), can be used as a template when creating new patterns showing a balanced geometric foundation.

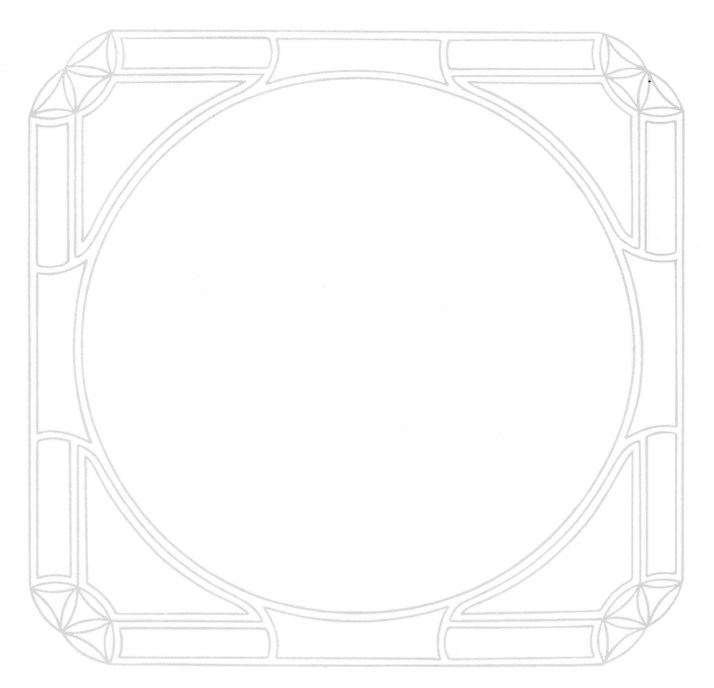

Templates

On the following pages various templates are included for perimeters or border designs. The centre in each case has been left blank for your own design. Using the symbols and techniques acquired throughout this book a further free style design can be constructed.

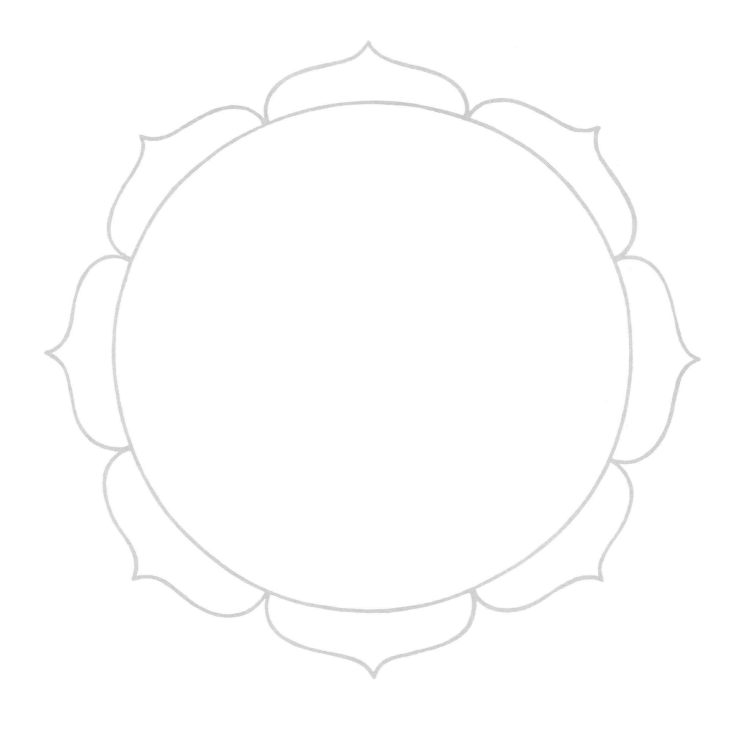

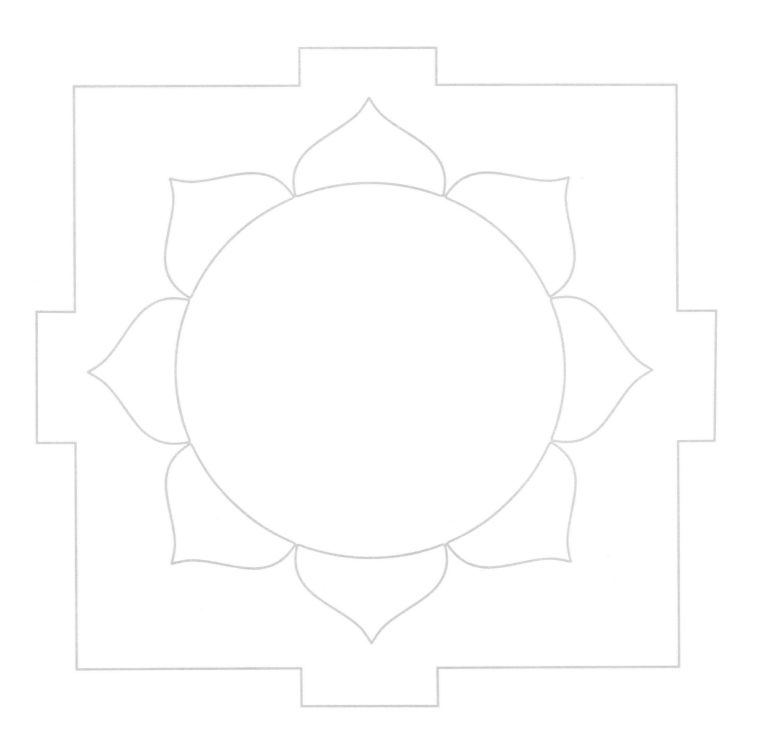

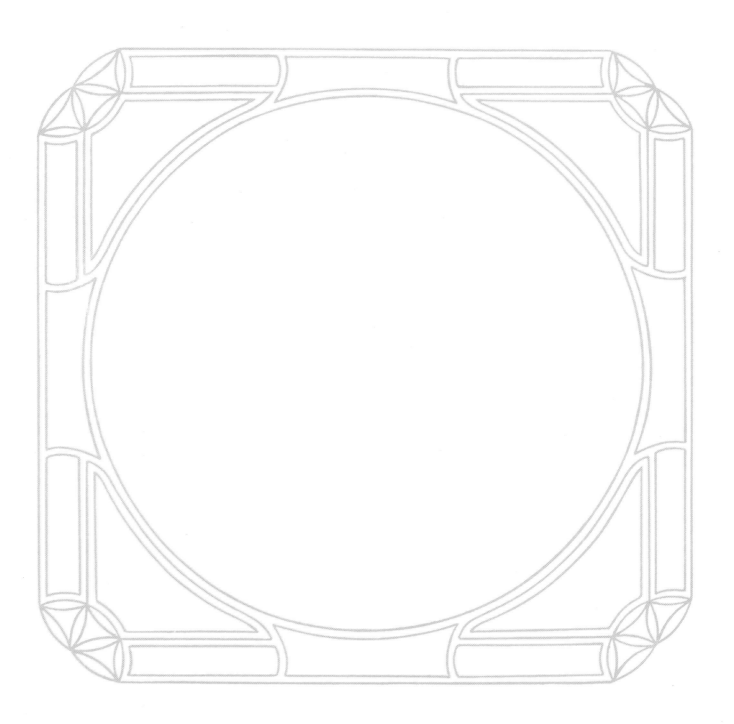

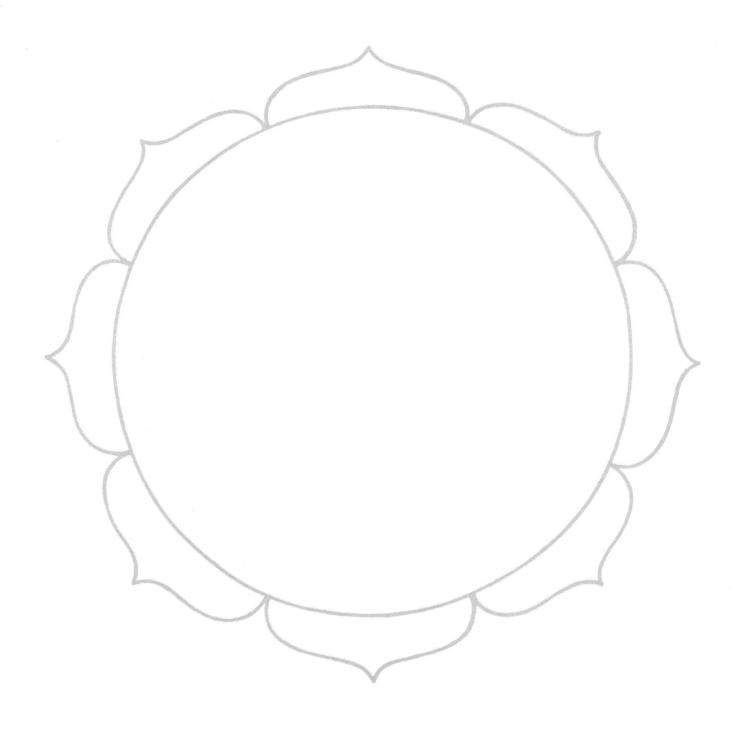

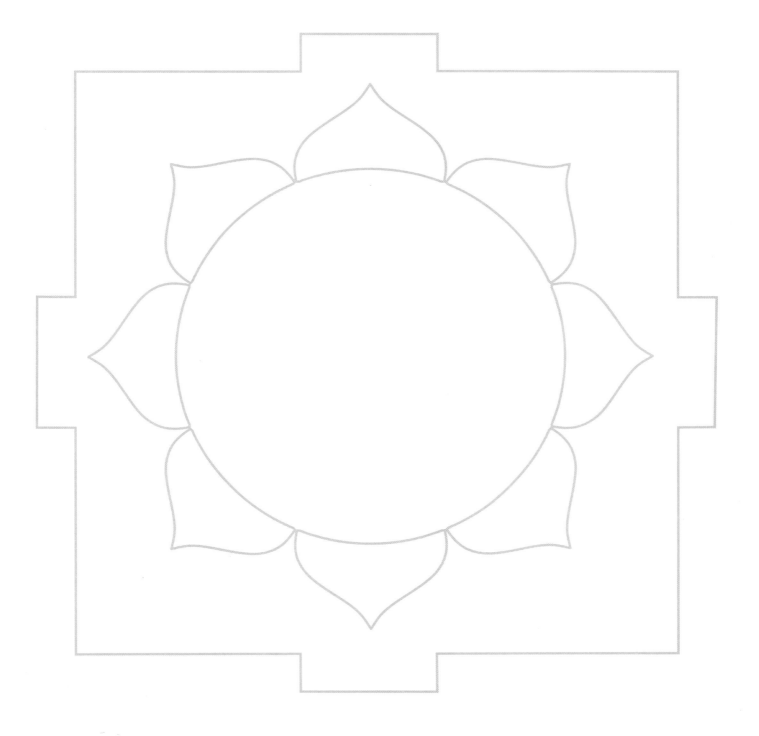